THE HAND OF GOD IN ALASKA

THE HAND OF GOD IN ALASKA

Jana Lee Johnson

XULON PRESS

Xulon Press
2301 Lucien Way #415
Maitland, FL 32751
407.339.4217
www.xulonpress.com

Printed in the United States of America.

ISBN-13: 9781545613375

"This is the day the Lord has made. Let us rejoice and be glad in it." (Psalm 118:24)

Did you know brown bears are also known as the Alaskan Grizzly? These two are playing in the water.

Brown bears will eat almost anything from bugs to berries, but plants are their main diet. When it's fishing season, the bears eat salmon and pack on weight for winter. Male bears grow up to nine feet tall and weigh up to 1,200 pounds. Females grow up to eight feet tall, and can weigh up to 800 pounds.

Alaska has three different species of bears: Brown, Black, and Polar. Brown bears are my favorite.

Brown bears usually hibernate from October through March. However, they never fully sleep. If you walk into a bear's den, it will open its eyes and look at you. If they feel threatened, they will get up to protect themselves.

Brown bears in the wild can live twenty-five or more years and they can run as fast as forty miles per hour.

The claws of a brown bear are straight and long; they use them to dig up insects or hold onto fish while they eat them. Can you guess how many fish they eat in a day? As many as they can catch!

All bear species are great, but which one is your favorite?

4

Caribou are also known as reindeer. Both males and females have antlers. The males grow much larger than the females. The adult bulls average 350-400 pounds. Adult females average 175-225 pounds. They like to eat mushrooms, leaves of willows, blueberries, and other tundra plants.

Jellyfish squirt water from their mouths and that moves them forward.

They sting their prey with long tentacles.

These two seagulls are standing on a floating log looking for some lunch.

This water bird is called a Common Murre. They can fly and float.

There are five different kinds of salmon in Alaska, as well as many other species of fish. Here are some fresh caught Silver Salmon, Rock Fish, and Halibut.

God said, " Let the oceans swarm with living creatures, and let the flying creatures soar above the earth." (Genesis 1:20)

Moose eat vegetation. Did you know they don't have any upper front teeth? Calves stay with their mothers for about a year.

Did you know moose can close their nostrils when they stick their head underwater?

They are also great swimmers and can swim up to ten miles without taking a break.

If they are in a hurry, they can run as fast as thirty-five miles per hour.

Bulls lose their antlers in the winter, but they grow back in about five months.

Moose have long legs, so it makes it easier for them to walk in the snow in the winter, and wade in the water in the summer.

God made all creatures great and small, the Lord God made them all.

Sea Otters dive for food like shellfish or clams, and they use a rock as a tool to break open the shell while they eat floating on their backs. Then they wash themselves and take a midday nap. Sometimes they use sea kelp as an anchor by draping it over their bodies to keep from drifting away.

Did you know that bald eagles don't get their white head until they are between four and five years old? Their wingspan is 5.9-7.5 feet wide.

"But they who wait upon the Lord shall renew their strength, they shall mount up with wings of eagles." (Isaiah 40:31)

19

Alaska is the world's top fishing spot for salmon. While people are busy fishing, this Dungeness Crab washed up on the shore.

Did you know a squirrel's front teeth never stop growing, so they never wear out? Even after eating all those nuts!

Pretend you are hiking on this trail. What animal could be around the next corner? What would you like to see?

This beautiful plant is called Fireweed. Alaskans say when the blossoms reach the top, the first snowfall is only six weeks away.

These colorful birds are Sandhill Cranes. They have a six to seven-foot wingspan and fly in a V shape formation. They make a rattling, bugle sound.

"In His hands are all the depths of the earth, and the mountain peaks belong to Him." (Psalm 95:4)

Did you know beavers build dams to provide still, deep water to protect against predators, such as coyotes, wolves and bears?

The fishing boats are on their way for the adventure of the day.

"Come, follow me," Jesus said. "And I will make you fishers of men." (Matthew 4:19)

28

Halibut are a flat fish that are brown on top with an off-white underbelly. They can weigh over 400 pounds. Yum-yum!

Alaska is a lot of fun and called the Land of
the Midnight Sun. It's late at night and though
the sun is shining bright, it's time to go to bed
and rest our sleepy heads and say our evening
prayers. Thank you Lord for everything, the
mountains, sun and trees, but mostly, Lord,
thanks for making me!

Author-Photographer Jana Lee Johnson

Printed in the USA
CPSIA information can be obtained
at www.ICGtesting.com
LVHW051130191023
761545LV00013B/160